This Bridal Shower Guest Book Belongs To:

_____

_____

Name: Date:

_____

_____

Advice And Wishes:

_____

_____

_____

_____

_____

Name: Date:

_____

_____

Advice And Wishes:

_____

_____

_____

_____

_____

Name: Date:

_____

_____

Advice And Wishes:

_____

_____

_____

_____

Name: Date:

_____
_____

Advice And Wishes:

_____
_____
_____
_____
_____

Name: Date:
_____
_____

Advice And Wishes:
_____
_____
_____
_____
_____

Guest

Name: **Date:**

_____
_____

Advice And Wishes:

_____
_____
_____
_____
_____

Name: _____ Date: _____

_____

_____

Advice And Wishes:

_____

_____

_____

_____

_____

Name: Date:

_____

_____

Advice And Wishes:

_____

_____

_____

_____

_____

Guest

Name: Date:

_____

_____

Advice And Wishes:

_____

_____

_____

_____

_____

Name: Date:

Advice And Wishes:

Name: Date:

_____
_____

Advice And Wishes:

_____
_____
_____
_____
_____

Name: Date:

_____
_____

Advice And Wishes:

_____
_____
_____
_____
_____

Name: Date:

_____
_____

Advice And Wishes:

_____
_____
_____
_____
_____

Name: _____ Date: _____

_____
_____

Advice And Wishes:

_____
_____
_____
_____
_____

Name: Date:

_____

_____

Advice And Wishes:

_____

_____

_____

_____

_____

Name: Date:

_____
_____

Advice And Wishes:

_____
_____
_____
_____
_____

Name: Date:

_____

_____

Advice And Wishes:

_____

_____

_____

_____

_____

Name: **Date:**

Advice And Wishes:

Name: Date:

___

Advice And Wishes:

___

Name: **Date:**

_____

_____

Advice And Wishes:

_____

_____

_____

_____

_____

Name: Date:
_____
_____

Advice And Wishes:

_____
_____
_____
_____
_____

Name: Date:

Advice And Wishes:

Name: Date:

_____

_____

Advice And Wishes:

_____

_____

_____

_____

Name: Date:

_____
_____

Advice And Wishes:

_____
_____
_____
_____
_____
_____

Name: Date:

_____

_____

Advice And Wishes:

_____

_____

_____

_____

_____

Name: **Date:**

_____

_____

Advice And Wishes:

_____

_____

_____

_____

_____

Name: Date:

_____

_____

Advice And Wishes:

_____

_____

_____

_____

Name: Date:

_____

_____

Advice And Wishes:

_____

_____

_____

_____

_____

Name: **Date:**

_____

_____

Advice And Wishes:

_____

_____

_____

_____

_____

Name: Date:

Advice And Wishes:

Guest

Name: Date:

_____

_____

Advice And Wishes:

_____

_____

_____

_____

_____

Name: Date:

_____

_____

Advice And Wishes:

_____

_____

_____

_____

_____

Guest

Name: **Date:**

_____

_____

Advice And Wishes:

_____

_____

_____

_____

Guest

Name: Date:

_____

_____

Advice And Wishes:

_____

_____

_____

_____

_____

Name: Date:

_____

_____

Advice And Wishes:

_____

_____

_____

_____

_____

Guest

Name: **Date:**

_____

_____

Advice And Wishes:

_____

_____

_____

_____

_____

Name: _____ Date: _____

_____

_____

Advice And Wishes:

_____

_____

_____

_____

_____

Guest

Name: Date:

_____

_____

Advice And Wishes:

_____

_____

_____

_____

_____

Name: Date:

_____

_____

Advice And Wishes:

_____

_____

_____

_____

_____

Guest

Name: Date:

_____

_____

Advice And Wishes:

_____

_____

_____

_____

_____

Name: Date:

_____

_____

Advice And Wishes:

_____

_____

_____

_____

_____

Guest

Name: Date:

_____

_____

Advice And Wishes:

_____

_____

_____

_____

_____

Name: Date:

_____

_____

Advice And Wishes:

_____

_____

_____

_____

_____

Guest

Name: **Date:**

_____

_____

Advice And Wishes:

_____

_____

_____

_____

_____

Name: Date:

_____

_____

Advice And Wishes:

_____

_____

_____

_____

_____

Name: Date:

Advice And Wishes:

Guest

Name: **Date:**

_____

_____

Advice And Wishes:

_____

_____

_____

_____

_____

Name: Date:

_____

_____

Advice And Wishes:

_____

_____

_____

_____

_____

Name: Date:

_____

_____

Advice And Wishes:

_____

_____

_____

_____

_____

Guest

Name: Date:

_____

_____

Advice And Wishes:

_____

_____

_____

_____

_____

Name: Date:

_____

_____

Advice And Wishes:

_____

_____

_____

_____

_____

Name: Date:

_____

_____

Advice And Wishes:

_____

_____

_____

_____

_____

Name: Date:

_____

_____

Advice And Wishes:

_____

_____

_____

_____

_____

Name: Date:

_____

_____

Advice And Wishes:

_____

_____

_____

_____

_____

Name: Date:

_____

_____

Advice And Wishes:

_____

_____

_____

_____

_____

Name: **Date:**

_____
_____

Advice And Wishes:

_____
_____
_____
_____
_____

Name: Date:

_____

_____

Advice And Wishes:

_____

_____

_____

_____

_____

Name: Date:

___

Advice And Wishes:

___

Name: Date:

_____

_____

Advice And Wishes:

_____

_____

_____

_____

_____

_____

Name: Date:

_____
_____

Advice And Wishes:

_____
_____
_____
_____
_____

Name: Date:

_____

_____

Advice And Wishes:

_____

_____

_____

_____

_____

Name: Date:

_____

_____

Advice And Wishes:

_____

_____

_____

_____

_____

Name: Date:

_____

_____

Advice And Wishes:

_____

_____

_____

_____

_____

Name: Date:

_____
_____

Advice And Wishes:

_____
_____
_____
_____
_____

Name: Date:

_____

_____

Advice And Wishes:

_____

_____

_____

_____

_____

Name: **Date:**

_____
_____

Advice And Wishes:

_____
_____
_____
_____
_____

Name: Date:

_____

_____

Advice And Wishes:

_____

_____

_____

_____

_____

Name: Date:

_____

_____

Advice And Wishes:

_____

_____

_____

_____

_____

Name: Date:

_____

_____

Advice And Wishes:

_____

_____

_____

_____

_____

Name: Date:

_____
_____

Advice And Wishes:

_____
_____
_____
_____

Guest

Name: Date:

_____

_____

Advice And Wishes:

_____

_____

_____

_____

Name: **Date:**

_____
_____

Advice And Wishes:

_____
_____
_____
_____
_____

Name: Date:

_____

_____

Advice And Wishes:

_____

_____

_____

_____

_____

Guest

Name: Date:

_____

_____

Advice And Wishes:

_____

_____

_____

_____

Name: Date:

_____

_____

Advice And Wishes:

_____

_____

_____

_____

_____

Guest

Name: Date:

_____

_____

Advice And Wishes:

_____

_____

_____

_____

_____

Name: Date:

_____

_____

Advice And Wishes:

_____

_____

_____

_____

Name: **Date:**

_____
_____

Advice And Wishes:

_____
_____
_____
_____
_____

Name: Date:

_____

_____

Advice And Wishes:

_____

_____

_____

_____

_____

Name: Date:

_____

_____

Advice And Wishes:

_____

_____

_____

_____

Name: Date:

_____

_____

Advice And Wishes:

_____

_____

_____

_____

_____

Guest

Name: Date:

_____

_____

Advice And Wishes:

_____

_____

_____

_____

_____

Guest

Name: Date:

_____

_____

Advice And Wishes:

_____

_____

_____

_____

_____

Guest

Name: **Date:**

_____
_____

Advice And Wishes:

_____
_____
_____
_____
_____

Name: Date:

_____

_____

Advice And Wishes:

_____

_____

_____

_____

_____

Name: **Date:**

_____

_____

Advice And Wishes:

_____

_____

_____

_____

_____

Name: Date:

_____

_____

Advice And Wishes:

_____

_____

_____

_____

_____

Name: Date:

_____
_____

Advice And Wishes:

_____
_____
_____
_____
_____

Guest

Name: Date:

_____

_____

Advice And Wishes:

_____

_____

_____

_____

_____

Name: Date:
_____
_____

Advice And Wishes:
_____
_____
_____
_____
_____

Name: Date:
_____
_____

Advice And Wishes:
_____
_____
_____
_____
_____

Name: Date:

_____

_____

Advice And Wishes:

_____

_____

_____

_____

_____

Name: Date:

_____

_____

Advice And Wishes:

_____

_____

_____

_____

_____

Name: Date:

_____

_____

Advice And Wishes:

_____

_____

_____

_____

_____

Name: Date:
_____
_____

Advice And Wishes:
_____
_____
_____
_____

Name: Date:

_____

_____

Advice And Wishes:

_____

_____

_____

_____

_____

Name: Date:

_____

_____

Advice And Wishes:

_____

_____

_____

_____

_____

Name: Date:

_____

_____

Advice And Wishes:

_____

_____

_____

_____

_____

Name: Date:

_____

_____

Advice And Wishes:

_____

_____

_____

_____

_____

Name: Date:

_____

_____

Advice And Wishes:

_____
_____
_____
_____
_____

Name: Date:

_____

_____

Advice And Wishes:

_____

_____

_____

_____

_____

Name:	Date:

_____
_____

Advice And Wishes:

_____
_____
_____
_____
_____

Name: Date:

_____

_____

Advice And Wishes:

_____

_____

_____

_____

_____

Name: Date:

_____

_____

Advice And Wishes:

_____

_____

_____

_____

_____

Name: Date:

_____

_____

Advice And Wishes:

_____

_____

_____

_____

_____

Name: Date:

_____
_____

Advice And Wishes:

_____
_____
_____
_____
_____

Name: Date:

_____

_____

Advice And Wishes:

_____

_____

_____

_____

_____

Name: Date:

_____

_____

Advice And Wishes:

_____

_____

_____

_____

_____

Name: Date:

_____

_____

Advice And Wishes:

_____

_____

_____

_____

_____

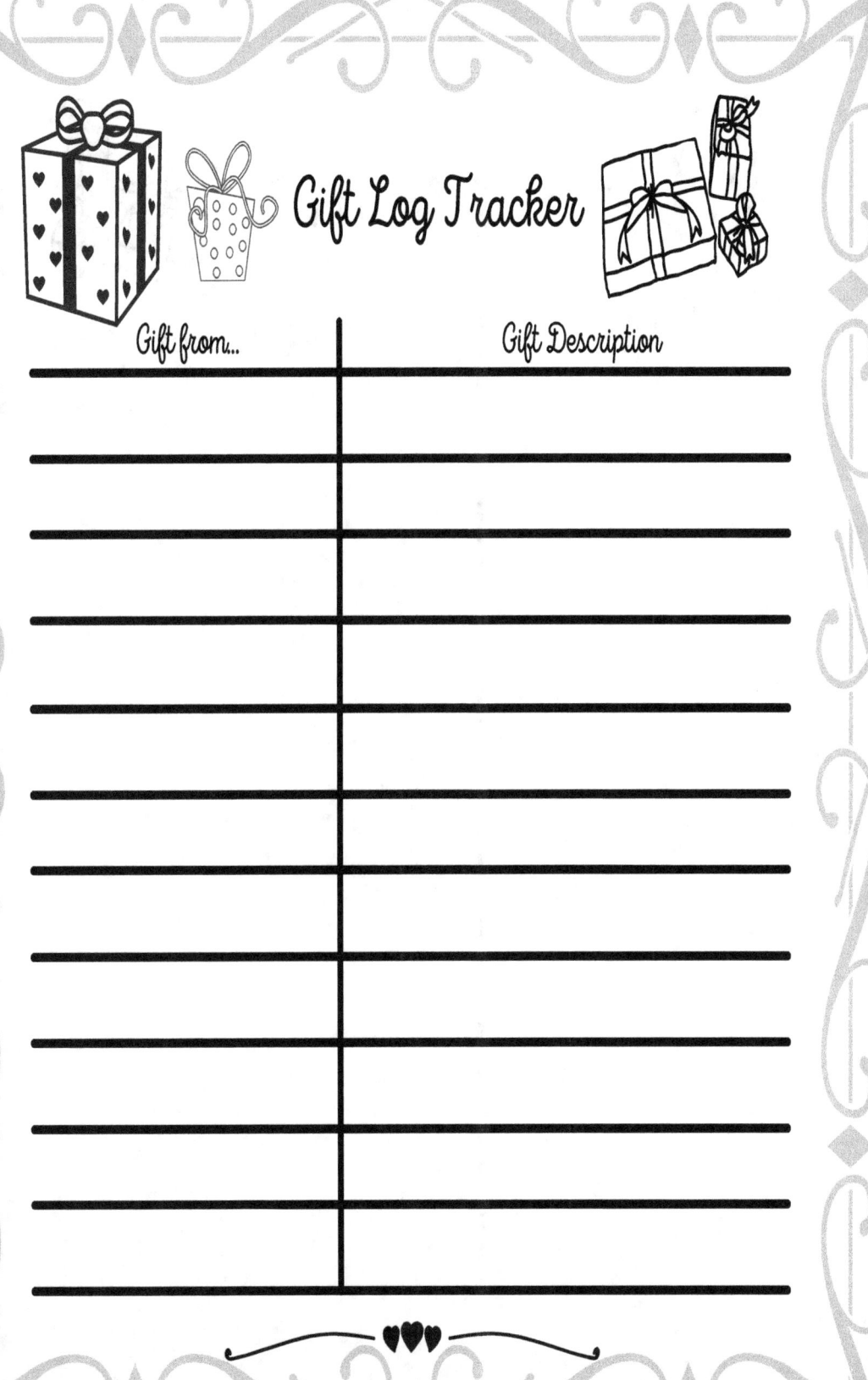

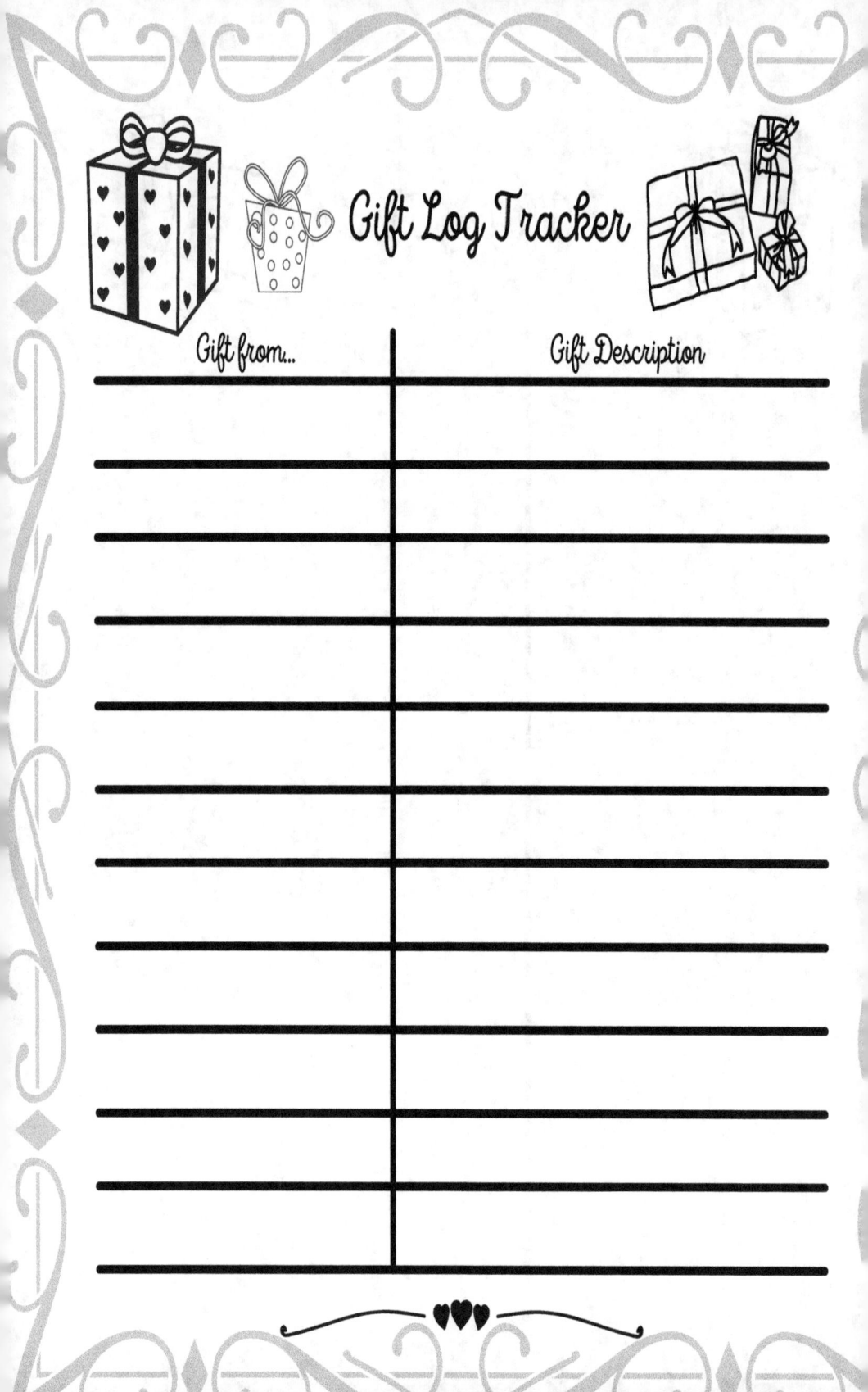

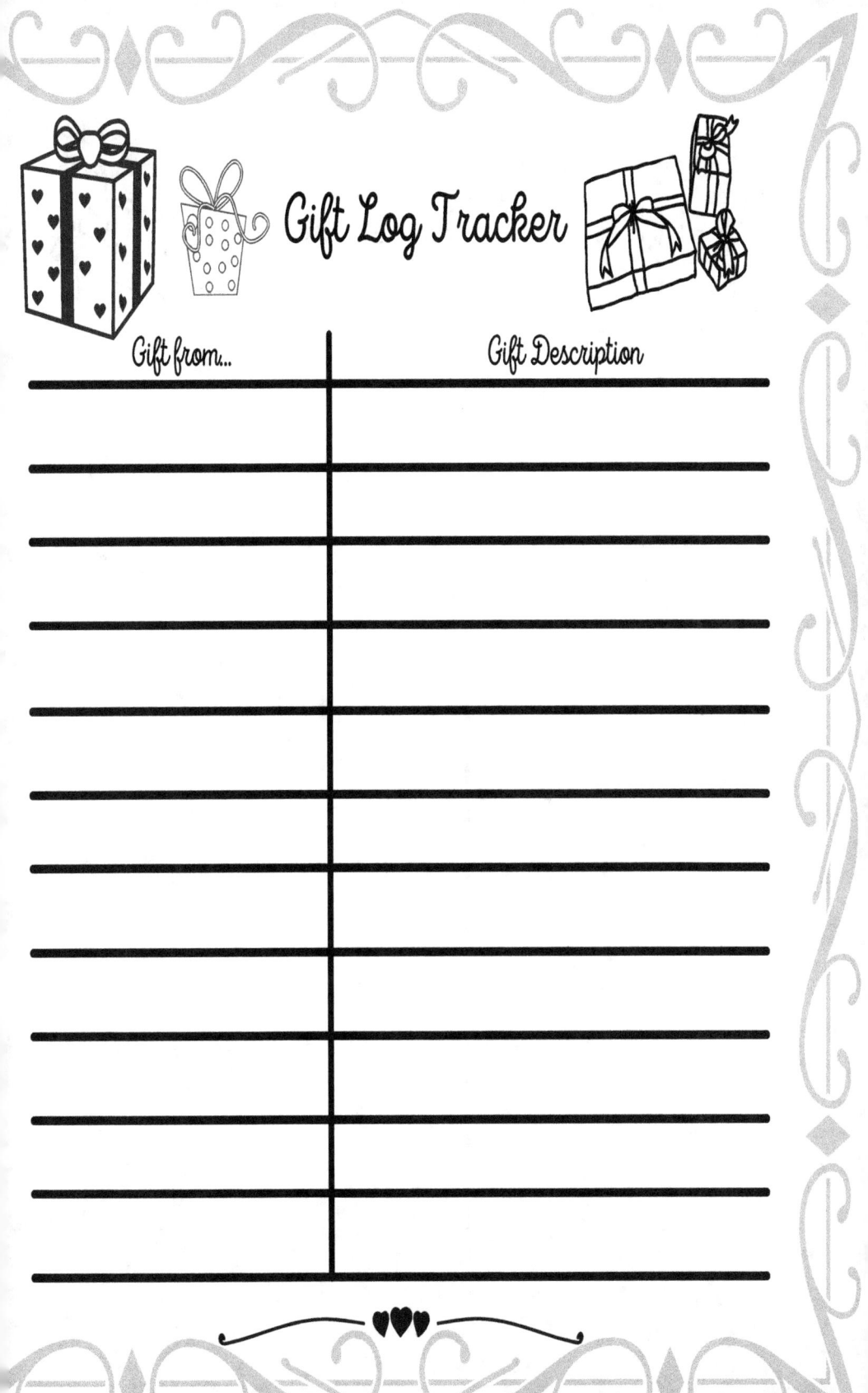

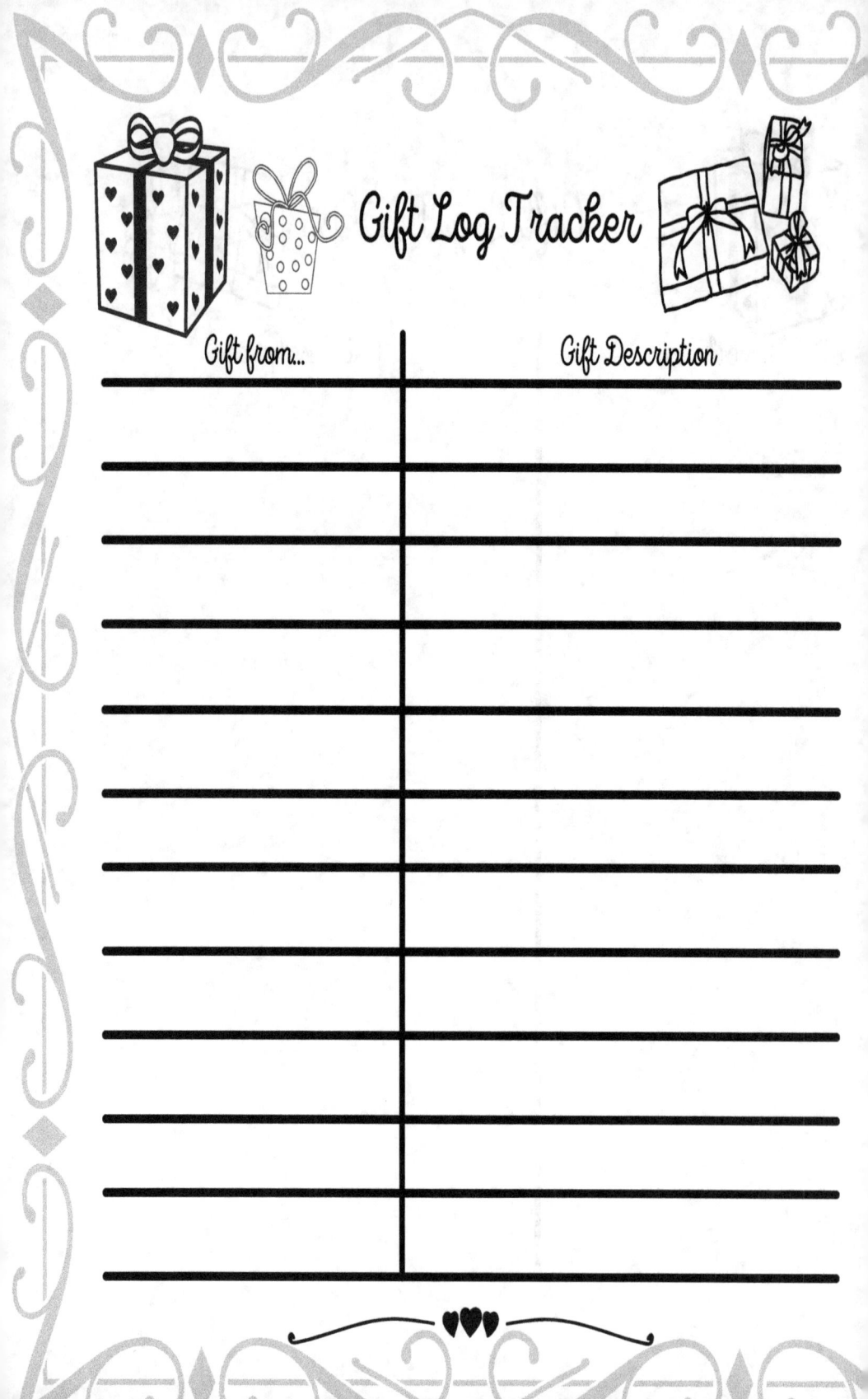

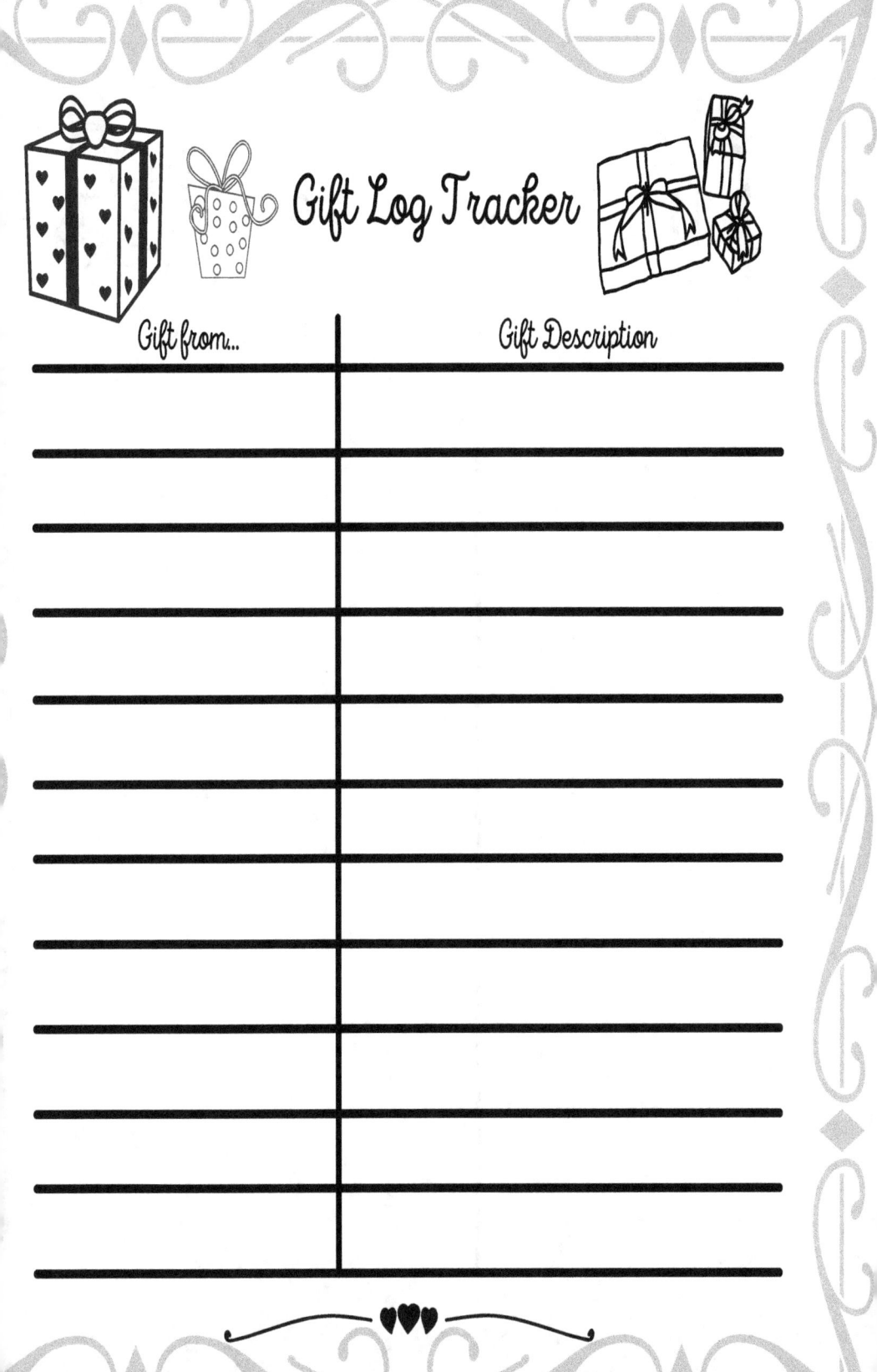

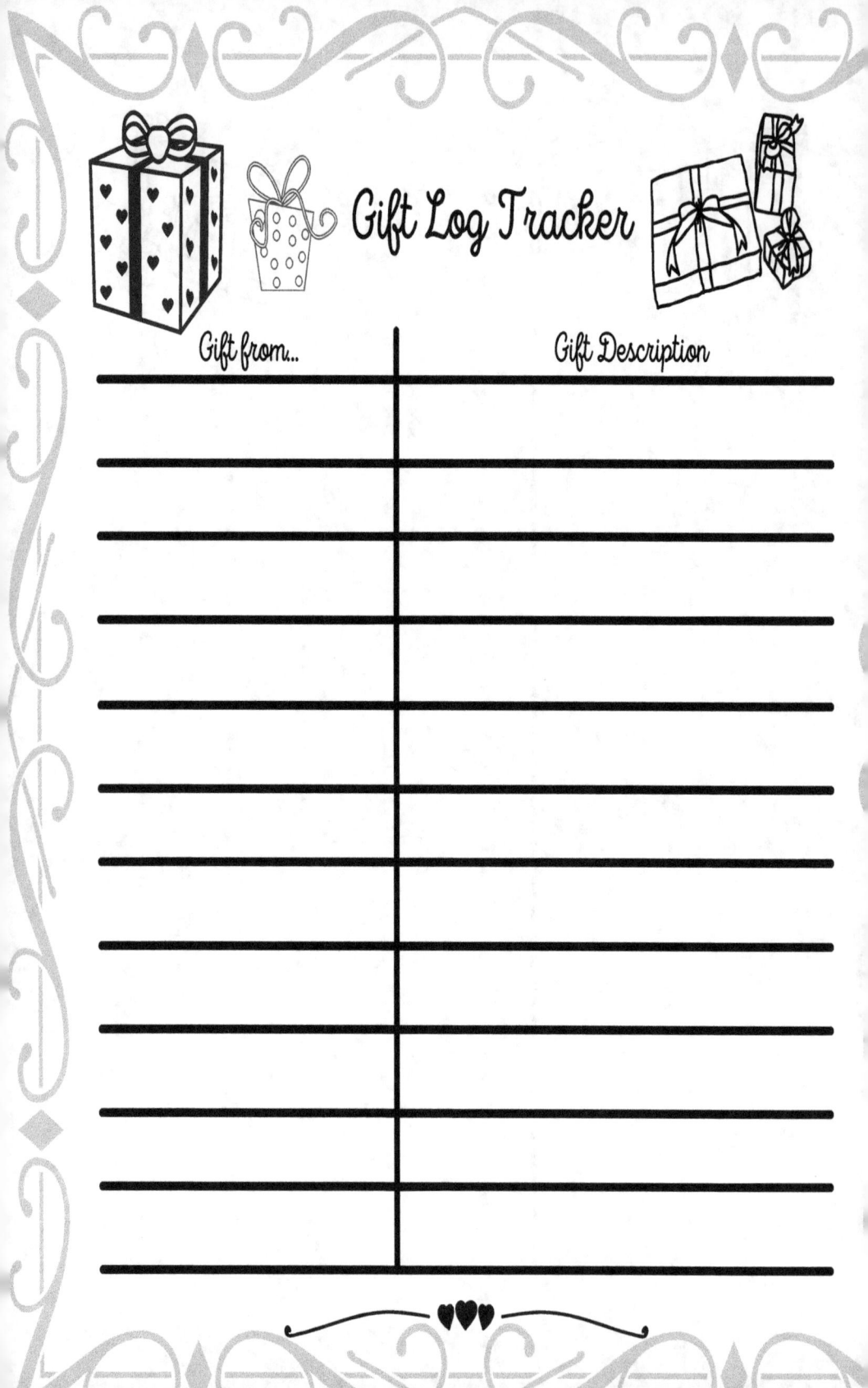

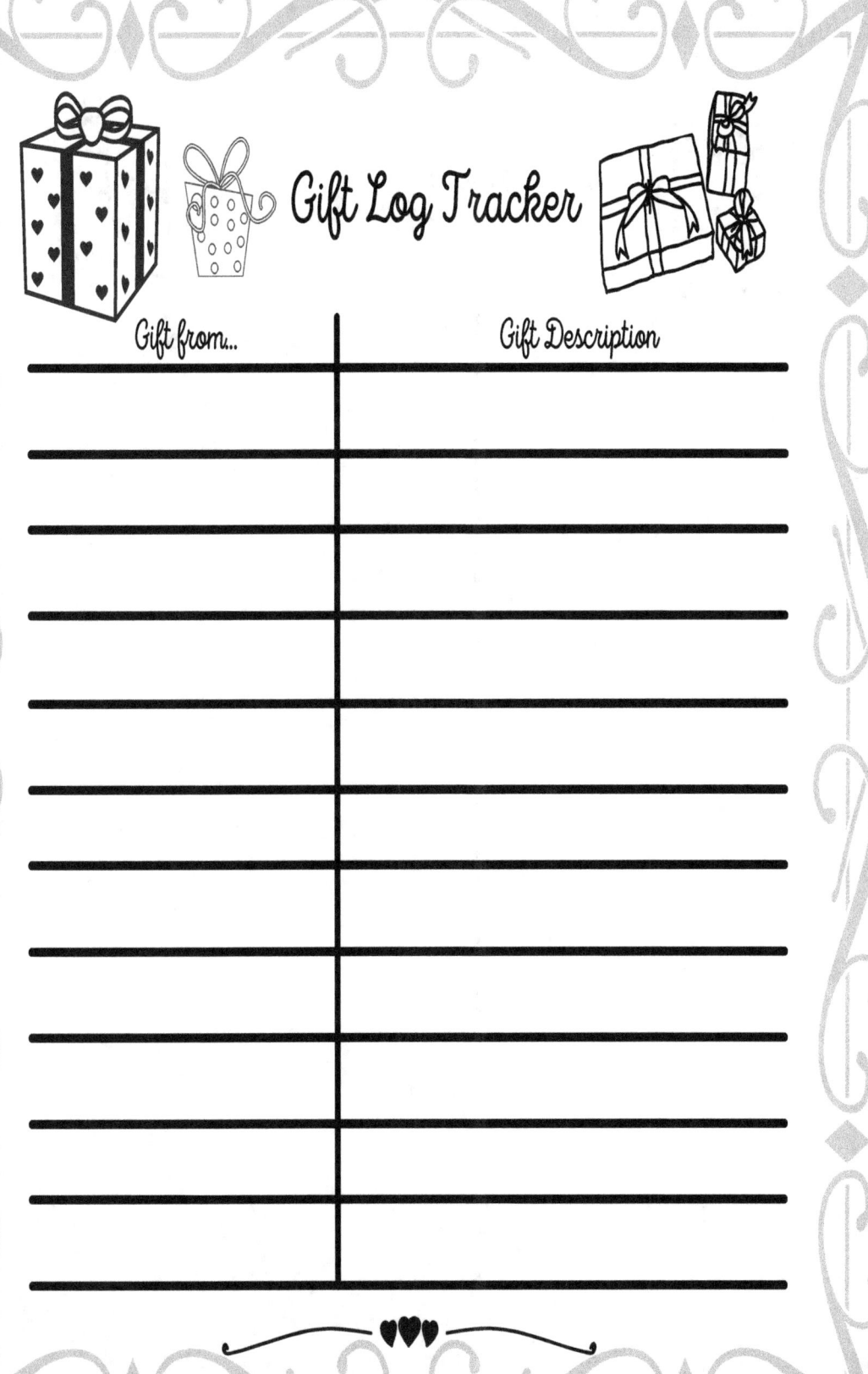

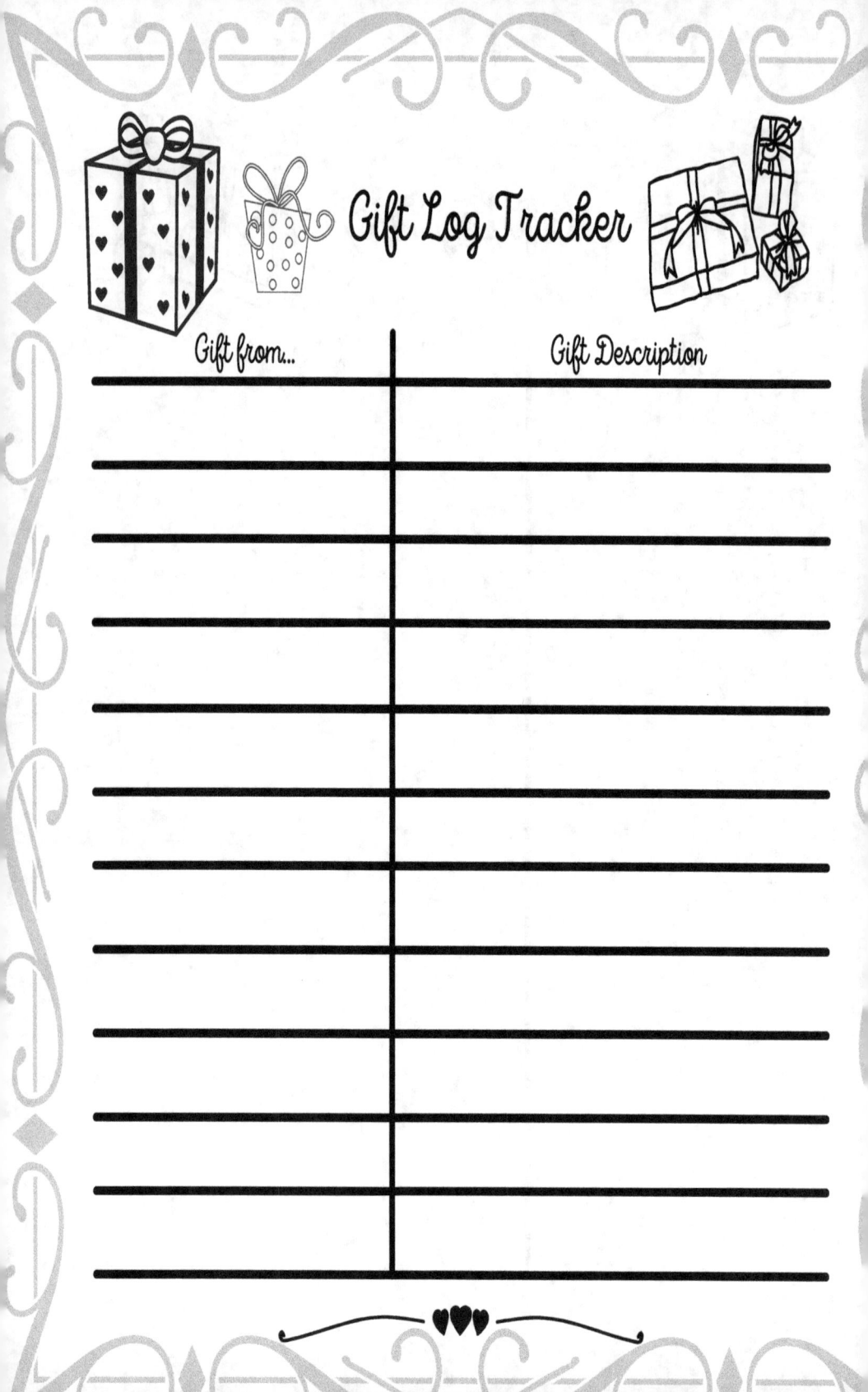

Copyrights
@ 2022
All rights reserved

You may not reproduce, duplicate, or send the contents of this book without direct written permission from the author. You cannot hereby despite any circumstance blame the publisher or hold him or her the legal responsibility for any reparation, compensation or monetary forfeiture owing to the information included herein, either in a direct or indirect way.

Legal Notice: This book has copyright protection. You can use the book for personal purpose. You should not sell, use, alter, distribute, quote, take excerpts or paraphrase in part of whole the material contained in this book without obtaining the permission of the author first.

Disclaimer Notice: You must take note that the information in this document is for casual reading and entertainment purpose only. We have made every attempt to provide accurate, up to date and reliable information. We do not express or imply guarantees of any kind. The person who read admit that the writer is not occupied in giving legal, financial, medical, or other advice. We put this book content by sourcing various places.

Please consult a licensed professional before you try any techniques shown in this book. By going through this document, the book lover comes to an agreement that under no situation is the author accountable for any forfeiture, direct or indirect, which they may incur because of the use of material contained in this document, including, but not limited to, - errors, omissions, or inaccuracies.

Thank You!

so much for trying our

Bridal Shower Guest Book

We'd love to hear from you!

If you've found this to be a good book please support us and leave a review.

If you have any suggestions or issues with this book, or if you want to test some of our latest guest books please email us.

Send email to:

pickme.readme@gmail.com